Blue Rust

T0079888

Books by Joseph Millar

Fortune
Overtime
Blue Rust

Blue Rust

Joseph Millar

Carnegie Mellon University Press
Pittsburgh 2012

Acknowledgments

Alaska Quarterly Review: "Fire"; *American Poetry Review:* "Year of the Ox," "For Weldon Kees," "Ocean"; *Ascent:* "Marriage"; *The Cortland Review:* "The Women of Poetry"; *The Fortnightly Review:* "Ginsberg"; *Grist:* "Native," "Divorce"; *New Letters:* "Judas's Mother"; *The Normal School:* "Labor Day"; *Ploughshares:* "Late December"; *Poet Lore:* "Who Do You Love"; *Poetry International:* "Urban Coyote"; *Raleigh Review:* "Half Made"; *River Styx:* "The Dutch Roll"; *Shenandoah:* "Lorca in California"; *Silk Road:* "Michigan Autumn"; *The Southern Review:* "Stove"; *Tin House:* "Shirt"; *Willow Springs:* "Sentimental," "Ginsberg," "Night Watchman"

The following poems appeared as a special supplement in Volume 10 of *The Idaho Review:* "Blow Job Cole Slaw," "Legacy," "Leaving Coos County," "Honeymoon," "Nightbound," and "For Annie."

The following poems appeared in the chapbook *Bestiary* published by Red Dragonfly Press: "Urban Coyote," "Day of the Dead," "Sentimental," "Lorca in California," and "Year of the Ox."

"For Weldon Kees" also appeared in the anthology *Aspects of Robinson*, edited by Christopher Buckley and Christopher Howell.

"Ocean" also appeared in a limited edition from Tavern Books of Portland, Oregon, edited by Carl Adamshick and Michael McGriff.

Thanks to the Virginia Center for the Creative Arts where some of these poems were written. Thanks also to the faculty, staff, and students of Pacific University's MFA program. Thanks especially to Dorianne Laux, Marvin Bell, Peter Everwine, Gerald Costanzo, Tim McBride, Shelley Washburn, Cynthia Lamb, the Dickman brothers, Michael McGriff, Alan Shapiro, Christopher Howell, Tony Hoagland, Ellen Bass and Janet Bryer, Nancy Hechinger, John-Roger, and John Morton.

Book design by Victoria Adams

Library of Congress Control Number 2011926207
ISBN 978-0-88748-549-7
Copyright © 2012 by Joseph Millar
All rights reserved
Printed and bound in the United States of America

10 9 8 7 6 5 4 3

Contents

One

Two

Three

Four

For my children:

Joe, Tiffy, Jess, and Daniel

It lies upon us to undo the lie
of living merely in the realm of time.
　　　　　　　—Theodore Roethke

Earlier, blue animals,
beyond me, light blue night . . .
　　　　　　　—Pablo Neruda

Rust never sleeps.
　　　　　　　—Neil Young

One

Nativity

Long after daybreak they were still trying
to deliver me, the birth blood dropping
on the hospital tiles, glittering under the lights.
I saw my father's corporal's stripes,
his tan army shirt that smelled of tobacco,
I heard the cold wind no one remembers
pouring down out of Canada.

My mother wrapped me up in her robe
fragrant with camphor and sweat,
hushing my desolate howls.
She loved me and she hated me
through those early months
when I wanted everything she had,
and all my father wanted
aside from her warm, pale body,
was to finish his hitch and get
the hell out of the army forever.

Each morning fine grains of salt
glinted like ice on the kitchen table
and like the insatiable mammal I was
I fastened onto her chafed, dark nipples.
They named me Rent Money
because I didn't pay any,
they named me Popsicle, Little Tongue, Gasser.
In August the Japanese surrendered
and he mustered out in Wisconsin.
We headed east in a '38 Studebaker,
its big engine swallowing the miles

of America, wheat fields and highway,
Chicago and Cleveland,
and they named me So Long
It's Been Good to Know You.

Donut Shop Jukebox

Each morning Willis plays checkers
with Eddie, the meth addict 40 days clean
who says he can see the board's white fibers
running from square to square.
Inside it smells of coffee and sugar,
The Shirelles singing Baby It's You
and someone taps on the fogged-up
window, late for work, needing
jumper cables. In the fields beyond
where the ditch runs with water
the star thistle opens its stunned
furry leaves, dry needles jabbing the air.

I like the engine roaring to life, a savage
red dogwood shedding its flowers
over the sidewalk, over the fence.
I like your hat with its purple feather,
cheap as a melody, cheap as a wish.

Year of the Ox

Now the town sleeps in its burial robes
its dim lace of snow trailing over the rooftops,
over the train station, over the struts
on the hotel catwalk
into the dark new moon.

In my boots and my lucky red sweater
I'm going to walk right up to the Ox-King,
touch the bell of his throat, his nostrils,
his thick breath sweet as new grass . . .
I'm going to ask him about the cold wind
shedding its seedpods and broken stems
over the garden we left behind,
where another man and woman
yoked together like us
sleep now on the back porch, the new
bamboo pressing up through the mud.

I can hear the sea calling out
from beyond the jetty, smell the pines
near the flooded-out bridge where today
someone tried to winch an old Volkswagen
up from the swirling waters.
Far down the coast the same west wind
blows through the marshes and river mouth
where my brother's boat rocks on its mooring.
He's the only one awake, modest and reliable,
replacing a frayed hose, tightening the clamps.
He doesn't trust the government
shining his trouble-light into the darkness,

his radio tuned to a satellite
broadcasting through the blue dust of space.

Ode to the Ear

This one's for you, winged skull-blossom
opening into the world, for the gold post held
in your fleshy lobe, for the ledges of blood
swollen inward. Here's
to the whirling sounds of the wind
spilling the dead crape-myrtle leaves
over the hedgerow and garden.
I heard the clock tower's
thick tones reach
into the blue void of Sunday
where I faltered, thinking of winter,
the past with its sunset-rouged face,
its décolletage and long opera gloves,
absinthe and tap water, fireplace
and roof gable, French doors
shedding the rain.

Why should it bring such comfort,
listening to typing in the next room,
the lost notes gathered and tended?
The right ear faces up in the darkness,
here's to its fluids and delicate tympani,
here's to its waxes and hairs,
helpless to close out this rhythmic tapping
it listens and hears and believes.

Romance

Soon the cold daylight turns its back
and we crewmen step into the skiff
carrying our groceries and motor oil,
your narrow face a blotch in the fog,
the banks of the estuary loosening
into the channel, horizon angling west.
One more month coming up
watching the moon in its changes
hoping the salmon will finally arrive,
one more month listening
to seabirds and wind,
listening to you dreaming out loud
about the waitress in Naknek
who called you Honey
when she brought the eggs
thinking because of your red moustache
you might be one of the Russians
with their slick fiberglass Wegley boats
we never understood how they could afford.

You could have made a life with her, you said
as we watched the cork line
straighten and drift.
You could settle down by her woodstove
turning your back to the road outside,
hidden away in her kitchen,
smelling the spaghetti sauce
like a child or an old man. You could
live easy and die happy, a candle burning
in every window, the blue compass needle

and hands of the clock pointing north
through the field's wavy grass.
You could make your grave in her.

Divorce

If you were as tired as I was
you too might want to lie down
with the anonymous cats of Santa Cruz
under the gray cars in the parking lot
where the Catholic church
spreads its burnt shadow
shadow of blood, shadow of thorns—

you could sleep in your overcoat
for maybe three days
like Villon or John Clare
trying to forget the rash on your arms
and the sleek androgynous judge
with a French actress's full upper lip,
his black hair marcelled close
to his skull, his necktie the green
of mosquito repellent.

Now the crickets are throbbing
the ancient psalm of tall grass.
You clasp both hands over your heart
with its pawnshop guitar and fake fur jacket,
its cloth roses sewn end to end,
the turquoise necklace you traded for money
so far from home and too late for autumn,
frozen star lilies bent to the ground.

The Dutch Roll

My father skates on ahead of me,
hands deep in his greatcoat pockets,
brown fedora jammed low.
He's showing me the Dutch Roll,
how to move down the ice for long distances
as they do in the Land of the Silver Skates
shifting one's weight from foot to foot
without thrusting the legs.
I'm proud of the way I can skate,
way better than my brothers.
We're headed for the covered bridge
two miles downstream to the east
and I watch his back. The fur
collar doesn't cover his ears
but he never seems to get cold.
French Creek will not freeze like this
for the rest of the winter we live here,
and tomorrow he'll start drinking again.
Willow branches thin as whips
hang down from the frozen banks,
blackberry canes and pieces of bark
encased in the ice's dark rind.
I smell the wool of my gray muffler,
my eyes are starting to sting. Every
so often the ice booms and cracks
like a rifle going off in a vault
and I hear my own blades
scrape and cut deep on the long thrust
pushing away, having abandoned
the rolling motion because I'm trying now

to catch up. My feet ache from the cold.
I don't want to chicken out and quit.
I don't know how the Dutch kids do it.
The woods are quiet and full of wind
and I think: some things sound better
in books than when you actually do them.
Maybe my father comes back for me,
and we turn and skate back upstream together
past the big rocks crusted with snow,
the ice so thick here I can't see through it.

Ginsberg

It was the time of the pin oak leaves
and the highjacked bus upside down
in the ditch. It was the spring
of 1970 and Ginsberg ate peaches from a can
and stroked each cow on its face
before leaving for DC on a plane
where the ghosts of four students
hung in the air like tear gas
over the huge angry crowds,
where he would sound his gutteral *aum*
across the White House south lawn
after the speeches ended, then
tell everybody to pick up their trash.
When the sun went down
the trouble started.
Chuck Berry was playing a half-empty armory
trying to pay down his tax bill,
someone set fire to a squad car outside
and we roamed the streets
half drunk with the night air
and the moon overhead
which we thought we could swallow,
its pale rocks and electric dust,
the shadowy lakes on its dark side,
though it was daylight in Vietnam,
land of rice paddies and ancient poetry,
land of the lotus pond hidden from sight,
its presence so hard to know.

Kiski Flats

Soon we'll be driving the black road
I left by, shining with mica
blistered with tar, the back porch
collapsed where we ate the charred onion rings
watching the Steelers on channel four,
the hatchet sunk deep in the workbench he left
to die in his bed behind the closed door.

It's no crime to be tired of the sun,
to be secretive, hiding your pain.
We peer now into the choppy rooms,
the windows wavy with age and rain.
Let the phone ring forever, let the mail
pile up. Let the dry nest fall apart,
stuck together with last year's mud
jammed in the eaves and shaped like a heart.

For Annie

You bring the sausage and lentil soup
to the long couch
where I'm watching baseball
the night after the famous poet
commits suicide in New York,
black cushions upholstered
by a recovering addict
who left for the city
as soon as we paid him.

You wash the clothes,
the Levis and socks, though they're
soon grimed with sweat, wash
the dust from the lilacs
thirsty and stressed,
the Dog Star staring straight
down in our yard. Someone
may drop by for a visit,
you tell me, knowing I'm not
the most eager host, feet
splayed out on the window sill,
shirt and shoes piled on the rug.

There's a song women sing
you know all the words to,
to make a child stop crying and sleep,
a song to make a grown man forget.

Stove

When the iron stove he was trying to move
to warm up his cramped study
toppled from the second-floor landing
and began to step down the ancient stairs
my father wrapped both legs around
its firebox, straining to hold it upright
and spare the walls from its flames.

He suffered second and third degree burns
they swaddled in light gauze and cortisone salve,
and he'd sit in a tepid slurry for hours
an open fifth by the tub, soaking
the bandages loose from his thighs
under the acid-green light.
He'd sweat on the newspaper, soggy
in his hands, bellow for ice or a cigarette,
and curse all of us "little bastards,"
nursing the whiskey's measure of pain
and damning the small cottage he'd saved:
orphanage, palace of summer.

Now he sleeps on, smelling of medicine,
forever deeper and wider, his legs
which once ran The Hundred in ten flat
float apart in the water. God
only knows how far from this world
the fins of his dream have carried him,
the ocean breathing outside in the night,
its metal voice blistered with fallen stars,
its pale fans opening and opening.

Nightbound

Your knuckles relax and your hands
open slowly each time you enter
the house of sleep
which you will never own,
its black windows shining
on the black lawn
smelling of cloves,
feathers and ink, the flakes
of soot collecting ceaselessly
over the smoldering cookfire,
perfect whorled thumbprint left behind
on the water glass by the sink.

Nothing to hear or see or hold onto,
blue rust floating away from your
touch, dark mosses crumbling under
your tongue, nothing to carry back,
curled on one side with your knees drawn up:
father, mother, grandmother, uncle,
naming your dead one by one.

Song for Stevie

Three days now since my friend died
whom the fever had worn thin,
thinner than even the cancer
thinner than methadone

and I want to lie down and sleep forty hours
on the dark sofa's thick woven flowers
upholstered by Oakland Bobby
who could never stay clean for long
with his stories of stolen rent money
and sidewalk romance gone wrong.

My friend helped me plant
the red flowering currant, he spaded
alfalfa meal into its roots,
what large family carries his ashes
west today to the Oregon coast?

What zodiac of faces will rise
misting the windows at Ocean Sky
where we ate Kung Pao chicken
the hotter the better
before going to hear Taj Mahal or Wayne Shorter
getting high on watery tea.

Tonight the earth sleeps wrapped in its mantle
smelling of pine tar and cinders
and stars keep burning their metal fires
far out over the sea

but no one knows for sure where he's gone,
the human one, the look in his eyes
watching the long grass sway by the beach,
the soul with its lit endless gaze.

Judas's Mother

Judas's mother misses her son, each night
she wanders the old road calling him,
headed for Galilee Beach. She remembers
the tortoise he kept in a box, the sandals
unlatched on the window sill, his big
knuckled hands building a fire, his knife
cutting bread at the evening meal.
Now her olive trees grow bent,
down on their knees in the dirt. It was
a mistake for him to leave home, thieves
and fishermen, stargazers, priests.
She thinks of his rusty hair and dark eyes:
Judas of loneliness, Judas of pain,
Judas of misery and silent farewell.
Over her head the galaxy turns
once around on its crooked stem.
Under her feet the long tracks
of wandering press down into the sand.

Two

Ocean

Where we swam alone under the skiff,
its green shadow knife-shaped
far overhead,
ribbons of seaweed,
the soundless engine,
soundless the shouts
and the wind
shouldering the surf's
white flowers,
water snuffed up our sinuses,
the beach-fire cinders
like phosphorous at night,
jeans caked with salt,
the funeral moon.
Beach with dark rocks and saw grass,
winter keeps coming down from the north,
each grain of sand ticks underfoot,
each star whines overhead.
Beach with dark rocks, the long boats
drift, the children leave home, no one
speaks. Each night lying down
in our sea-wrack, each day waking
into our skin.

* * *

Come close and whisper the names
of the living, names of the dead returning,
sleepwalkers holding their hands out,
litter of sea-straw and sand like dark metal,
song of arriving and going away.

Forgive me my pride, inexplicable
under the circumstances,
storm coming in tomorrow night,
old raingear dotted with herring scales.
I ate the kelp blossom
down to the root,
eel flesh and crab flesh, I ate the shark meat,
octopus, yellow fin, scallops, clams,
delicate flesh of the lobster.

★ ★ ★

What was the song she sang,
the sea lion cow asleep on a rock
near Point Reyes?
I hear the deep halls of water
filling up on the ebb
as she turns over, sighing into the algae,
slides back into the tide.
I squatted still in the autumn sand
thinking of red roe and black hair,
women gone down into themselves,
funky, brash,
croaking and thrashing
eyes staring blind as glass.

★ ★ ★

Don't be afraid to go sailing out,
don't think of riptides,
storms,
huge seas

risen over the fly bridge,
threads of fire,
the jaws of a wolf eel
slithering out of the trawl.

*   *   *

One summer night the fisherman told us
he'd run aground in the river mouth, hull
mired deep in black mud. He said he saw
the hour of his birth, the swamp slowly
filling with light, kelp stretched out
like a vestment covering the flanks of the marsh,
the sea's wretched age, monstrous and fecund,
hair full of dead leaves, rayed petals clustered,
shoals of dark gravel exposed.
Inside the wheelhouse one candle burning,
bunks tilted stiffly to starboard.

He told us sometimes he'd rather be dead
than face the gray rooming house
and a day-job, his heart like iron
remembering the sea and staring
at frayed pallets stacked in a warehouse
smelling of creosote. All
the gathered rubbings of shore trash
making him sneeze and itch:
stove-ashes, moth wings stuck to the screens,
dog hair, spider webs, elm pollen.

*   *   *

Always the sound of the hull slapping down
into the wave trough, always
the caulked seam of metal
its green wet-patch turning to sugar,
saltwater seeping down the spine,
miles offshore the snowy moonlight,
miles below the abyssal trench
where a creature with no eyes
and glandular poison sends its forked signals
into the murk, sleepless predator
prowling the blind shadows,
turning its stomach inside out,
vulnerable, sunk in its hunger.

★ ★ ★

This time of year you can hate the snow,
freezing the tie-up lines, coating the wharves,
falling into the jagged surf.
If you wait long enough you can ride
into town on the boom truck, its tire chains
shredding the crust, the engine
so noisy no one can speak,
the driver grinding it up into second
frowning with grease on his knuckle.

No place will be open now
except for the sad bar, barren of women,
except for the motel near the dunes
with its flocked wallpaper
and rusty heater that moans

in the night like a tired swan.
The next day no one will look
in your eyes, transparent stranger
belonging to no one,
not the children sledding on cardboard
down through the frozen parking lot,
not the waitress humming a song
you wish you could remember . . .

if she asked you about your family
you could show her their silhouettes
in a drop of saltwater
from Wingaersheek Beach
you keep in a jar by the window.
You could show her
the rags of evening
fluttering over the waves
and a sofa's blond fabric
dotted with burns
like the skin of a mangy leopard.
You could show her the plaster
Egyptian sculptures,
emblems of dynasty fallen,
its copy of Queen Nefertiti's face,
the nose broken off,
her green headdress wound high
into the domed light
sifting down on the sink.
Thy sea is so great
and my boat is so small

stamped in metal over the door—
my thin hands gripping the shovel
loosening dirt in the garden,
the restless claws of the ocean
turning the pebbles and rocks and sand,
tumbling the chitin and shell fragments
ceaselessly each day and night forever:
Quaternary, Cretaceous, Jurassic, Cambrian
onto the shores of this world.

Three

Shirt

The last day of 2008 I woke
wearing the same blue shirt I wore
driving down through the pines
to hear Carlos Santana,
the hills a pale brown near Vallejo
where Bill Graham's helicopter crashed
in the power lines over the marshland.

The shirt hung on a shovel near Big Sur
smelling of almonds and sulfur
where I sat one morning reading Chuang Tzu
trying to understand about the Tao.
I wore it to feed Amy's chickens.
and wrapped its loose arms
around my wife, who was smoking
outside by the mailbox, having swallowed
a fragment of glass in her coffee
the Advice Nurse said was most likely harmless,
trusting the colon's pulses to pass it
moment by moment.

We drove back north through Golden Gate Park
where an alligator once escaped
into the pond just off Lincoln Drive
and where Michael Bloomfield OD'd in his car
near the hall of flowers
and the Grateful Dead played for free.

We'd like to see them come back again,
the way Mickey Rourke showed up

at the Academy Awards interview
for his role as a broken-down wrestler
walking the two roads of grief and hilarity,
the cat's eye ring on his finger,
his silver tooth, his rat-goatee
and wraparound shades,
weeping into his water glass
mourning his dead Chihuahua:
I swear I'd give him the shirt off my back.

Urban Coyote

In the green dream of spring
I stretch myself out
letting the gray mist hide me
shoving my nose in the garbage pile
chewing egg shells and cheese rinds.
I swallow cellophane, I swallow cat hair,
butcher paper stained dark with fish blood
and run grinning through the blowsy woods
smelling the riverbank's plasma—
I smell the barns and the city dump,
the quail asleep in the tall grass.

In the morning the doctors send over
my lab results: triglycerides and cholesterol,
glucose and prostate antigen,
diets of cold fruit, nuts and water.
I sign the mortgage papers,
I read the bank statement,
I pay the gas bill, I sweep the floor

then in the marshy glycemic night
I lick back the plush fur covering my lips,
I steal whatever can fit in my mouth
under the fat April moon.

Breasts

This is the day the Lord has made
to write a poem about breasts

pointing high up in the twilit porches
of 1958, or falling loose facing outward

under a Mozart t-shirt
in the early Twenty-first Century,

the rustle and ticking of lingerie
nylon and silk and padded wire

rose-colored, flexible, layered and fine
on the third floor of Bloomingdale's,

its pavilion of dressing rooms platinum-colored,
curved like the hull of a ship.

Who Do You Love

This is the night after Bo Diddley died
and we sit in the café drinking iced tea
reading his lyrics in the newspaper
along with the story of the hairline crack
in the left front hoof of Big Brown,
another American original.
Outside the long cars prowl the dusk
trailing their ribbons of smoke,
heat lightning flickers over the street
and the waitress Arlene
brings salsa and chips.

I want to say thanks
for the cavernous voice
and the black cowboy hat,
the triangle rhinestone Fender guitar
and the scratchy beat everyone stole—
Quicksilver, Willie Dixon, The Who,
easy to shuffle to,
easy to dance to:
"walk 47 miles of barb wire
with a cobra snake for a necktie"
Chonk chicka chicka chonk chonk.

Fire

When Axel starts humping the Coupe de Ville's trunk
in Michael Cimino's The Deer Hunter
America raises its iron voice
over the coal fields of Pennsylvania:
backyard engine blocks, chain hoists,
bell housings, toothed gears
resting in pans of oil—stammering out
the poem of combustion,
bright tongues and wings, white-hot ingots
glimpsed in the huge mills by the river,
coke ovens, strip mines, brick stacks burning
over the spine of the Appalachians.

Carnegie, gifter of libraries,
Frick with his Rembrandts, his Titians,
both fast asleep in the arms
of the strikebreakers
under the ashes and slag.
Fire with no roots, no memory,
grooved steel running all night to Detroit,
fire of the profit line, fire of the shareholders,
I-beams, pistons, fenders and chrome.

Grandfather

The TV washes the house in blue light
needling out through the blinds

over the dead tomato plants, over the frozen roses.
They want us to take erection pills,

though our women have all passed
menopause, they want us to dye the gray

from our hair, they want us to go back
to high school. You don't see any TV cameras

following you along Queens Boulevard
and you don't care who you bump into

going to meet your new grandson,
aged thirteen days, the flesh of his face,

the palm of his hand moist and wrinkled
gripping the end of your finger, the pulp

of his scalp turning red as he cries
and you hold him against your chest.

Grandfather of time with no money,
grandfather of trash bins and hardboiled eggs,

sweeping the leaves from the driveway,
washing the iron pan.

You stroke his back hoping he'll burp for you,
hoping he'll puke on your shirt.

Late December

It's the day after Christmas
a flat gray morning where the rain
has fallen on the crooked streets
and no one has stolen our newspaper,
its headline denouncing the young Nigerian,
someone's devout beloved son
who tried to blow up a plane,
my own son half asleep on the couch
in his Levis and unraveled socks,
his brother still out looking for work
and the sound of coughing on the back stairs
like the ghost of Edna St. Vincent Millay.
Now the horses of North Carolina
bend down to drink
from their starry pond
having listened all night to the spacecraft
hovering like metal angels
over the fields and tobacco barns,
their plutonium shutters and platinum fins,
their calamitous holy light.

First Poetry
for Reed Fry

In our 21-year-old wisdom
we'd said it didn't seem that difficult
when the old painter spoke of the struggle
to keep facing empty canvases
and today I can hear the voice of the crow,
a manic exuberance wrapped in gauze
echoing over the yard.
I hear the neighbor:
Here Boomer, Here Boomer
calling his dog in the heat.

All of us sat quite still last week
in the Quaker meeting on Bath Pike,
neckties, dress shoes, and cars out front,
black and white photos on the wall:
you in your lineman's football pads
or a dark suit waiting to graduate,
though not one shot of the Hotel Holland,
its bare lightbulb hung
from a frayed wire, its SSI checks
and curry smells, overcoat and amphetamines.

It's a poet's right to take his own life,
so say the Roman Stoics, in a language
no one speaks any more
except for lawyers and priests,
but this was not your way
tortured by emphysema and bad kidneys
nor was it the way of your half-Sioux girlfriend
older than you by 20 years

enthroned in your bed in Room 213,
her gray braids unloosed, a tall Coors
in one hand, telling you
to turn down the doo-wop,
Little Anthony or The Dell Vikings,
the housefly on the windowsill
trying to mate with its shadow,
four of us playing Hearts on the rug.

At the airport I had to take off my jacket
and put my keys in a plastic tray.
I took off my shoes, took off my belt,
stepped through the twittering archway.
I gave them my jar of lime shampoo,
my shaving cream and my pen knife.
There's less of me to be afraid of
now that you're gone
though I remember the adolescent perfumes,
the first poems and communal wounds,
writing them down on the blank page:
the first times I felt the longing and pain
and hoped they'd remember our names.

1965 Triumph Bonneville

Which I paid for
with a loan from the bank
I skipped on four months later

and which I named Rosie
for its dark red frame,
its engine and twinkling spokes,

the transparent collage
faintly peach-colored
fiberglassed on its tank:

the zodiac and three faces
of Elvis, all four Beatles,
Fellini and Marx,

its dual concentric carburetors
impossible to keep synchronized,
its Rambler gas cap and Ceriani forks.

"Big English," which I rode through the hills,
the asphalt buzzing my hips and spine
outside Point Reyes where the fault line

runs straight down through Tomales Bay,
where the wind makes its sullen
unfathomable sounds.

Which I rode through the Mission
and through the Haight
which I rode by the sea in the rain

doing over a hundred half drunk
down Highway One
in a race with a Kawasaki.

Which was stolen in Golden Gate Park
while I made love in the rhododendrons
with a girl from Chicago named Vivian

who made me a velvet shirt
and probably saved my life
in those days before helmet laws

though she ended up moving to Santa Cruz
where she left me
for a Chinese surfer with an earring

and I hitchhiked back
through the country of Davenport
listening to the wind in the yellow grass,

the road unwinding silken, black,
the path alongside battered and dusty
under the bones of my feet.

Casting Type
for Scott King

He squats by the ancient flywheel
jiggling a piece of baling wire
into a tiny hole near the type carriage
and straddling an electrical motor—
untaped wires connected in series—
definitely not up to code.
He aims a squirt of silicone grease
under each side of the cross block,
slides in the matrix for a lower case "e,"
the most common letter in English, he tells me,
then fires up the gas torches
under the hot tin and lead:
this day an ornate Italian face
adapted from Jenson or the early Venetians,
its delicate joinings and curved serifs
more suitable for a sonnet or ode
than the woodcut likeness of Joe Hill
taped underneath the exhaust fan,
splash-marks of metal
belched from the melt pot
spangling his jacket and hat.

Marriage

You pick up a drop-forged claw hammer
then an axe with a steep shiny blade
saying This would be ideal
for striking one's husband 32 times
on his thick skull, like the woman
we watched on 48 Hour Mysteries
lying in our queen-size Posturepedic.
I'm thinking how fine
this free time together
looking for a can opener
the day of our anniversary,
to wander the tool shop
smelling the cold steel
packed in grease, implements
for joining and rending.
Now you hold up two
locking c-clamps, their jaws
heat-tolerant to 300 degrees.
We could be standing inside an airship
laughing and jostling each other
or inside a dead star
surrounded by metal, the whetstone's
fine oil, chisels and knives,
torches and welding tanks
rinsed in blue light, threaded light,
bridal light helplessly shining
over the spools of new copper,
over the pocked green lunar cement.

Lorca in California

Half the time I'm alone at night
when the raccoons come down to the yard,
rummage collectors, chewers of pine cones.
They sniff the flowers and the possum's carcass,
seething with the white mouths of death.

I grew tired of the poet dressed in black
like the night of no moon, the curved
balconies and colonnades, hothouse Madrid,
its old lacquer. I could care less about Dali now,
his glass clocks and corpses, his giant
moustache, or Buñuel's fake lenses
and flickering lights, all that bright equipment.

I want to stay here forever
in this ramshackle hut with its roses and dog hair,
its peach tree blossoms, pollen and dust,
the compost fuming out back by the fence.
My new lover works on the tuna boats,
he comes home smelling of old rope
and anchovies, money in both his front pockets,
shiny blue scales on his boots.

Honeymoon

The young bride drunk on champagne and reefer
bending too near our beach fire,

a bent Winston held in her lips,
singes both eyebrows a delicate gray.

The groom's passed out in a nearby hotel,
shuttered light from its TV ray

risen around him like swamp gas. He dreams
of Chinook salmon nosing upstream

to spawn in the gravel. The woman, just a girl,
keeps huddling close to my wife,

with no path out of the sawgrass,
the wedding guests vanished by late afternoon,

her sweater unraveling, crossed shoelaces
packed with wet sand and mud

while deep space opens over the beach,
quarks and novas, meteors, comets,

the black starry threshold raging behind her
breaking over the rocks.

Blow Job Cole Slaw

"A woman will give you anything,"
T.K. would advise, "if you know
how to cook." He'd lean against
the scarred cutting block, sleeves
rolled up past the elbow, chopping
the purple and ivory cabbage
we could only get once in a while
into narrow shreds. Some nights
I still dream of the salmon boat,
the picking-bin littered with black tape
and hanging twine, sunset turning
dim like a weld over the Bering Sea.

We chewed the fine roughage
gratefully along with our noodles
and corned beef hash, the net
a loose skirt flaring down
over the stern roller's horns.
So much vinegar, so much mayonnaise:
night coming up from the shifting depths,
its dark veils unwinding, its unbraided hair,
floating half a mile up the cutbank, we
slept in our damp socks and sweatshirts,
we opened our cramping, feverish hands.

Half Made

Something half made like the love poem
left behind in the front seat
or the youngest child who keeps turning
to leave, his nicotine fingers and widow's peak.
Something half made like this high rise,
jackhammer breaking the curb,
its terrace abandoned, then planted again
with lilacs and clumped, fleshy herbs.
Something half made like a wedding blanket
nobody thinks will last or it could be
the thin skin of the past:
counting the capillaries and veins,
the tiny bones in your feet,
even at night the blood pulses,
the iron planet hums in the heat.
Something half made
like the song of the crow,
the marriage vows given and taken
even at night, blow by blow.

Four

Leaving Coos County

We follow the trail's bleached
driftwood snags over the dunes
changing shape as we walk them,
around us the cries of wild birds
and the west wind blowing
the flat grass down,
grass of heaven, grass of the coast,
shin bone of a deer half hidden
there, its tendon still attached
to the darkened hoof, offshore
a trash barge towed
toward the dump.

What have I lost
in the sea's wide pastures
watching for whales headed south?
Goodbye to the salmon
swerving and thrashing
upstream to spawn and die.
Goodbye to the sky turning dark
at 4:30, gray rain falling
for weeks in the sloughs,
goodbye to the child
jumping over the puddle,
the moon eclipsed in the red
earth-shadow over the Chinese restaurant,
dark pines grown down
close to the road.

Goodbye to the shipwreck
unwrapped by the storm,
trapped in its hollow bed.
Goodbye to the hunting knife
shaped like a fish
that cut the frayed tow rope free.

Legacy

The onions have shed their papery skins
in the basket next to the sink
and the acacia's unhooked its bent gray
stems from the freezing backyard mud.
Now that I've cleared the ice from the gutters
maybe the world won't expect too much
with its ostrich skin dashboard and heated seats,
its Cadillac rims and wing mirrors.
I leave them the dark coat I stashed in the truck
working overtime Friday nights
then put on over Levis and shirt
to pay my respects to Jackie McLean
from the cafe tables at Yoshi's.

Let them have the cramped apartment
now that the rents have doubled again,
the broken stairs and cracked sidewalk,
children's drawings: fishes and trees
chalked in purple, half washed away.
So many mornings of rain and exhaust,
so many footsteps, so much harsh breath,
so many waves breaking uncontrollably
over the winter piers. I could
never stop you from leaving, cars
in the ditch, black ice on the levees,
mornings the fog sank down and froze
and the dawn came up white as dust
over the bushes and cinders,
over the ragged beach, over the kitchen
crowded with smoke, the laughter we ate like bread.

Sentimental

I'm writing this down with a pen from Rite-Aid
which no one gave me and I did not steal
my hand curved over itself
like the claw of a possum
following the late November light
into the woods where Tolstoy was buried.

Me and James Wright sit down by a red pine,
watching a wiry dog chase the crows
and hoping the rain will hold off.

We speak of the smell of certain saloons,
the bar lit gold by glasses of beer,
the dartboard and shuffleboard,
the mirrors and coats and the women's dark hair.

We talk of the high school field's cut grass,
the tough skin of the tackling dummy—
stopping every so often
to take a swallow of water and lime—
the fresh landscape of a woman's back,
the Ohio River sucking its banks.

We talk of Li Po and Vallejo,
of telling the critics to stick the shield
of irony up their ass
and the three policemen
who appeared at Tolstoy's funeral
whom the crowd forced to show
respect for the dead,

who took off their hats
and knelt down in the leaves.

The Women of Poetry

for DL and NH

I never wanted a red sports car
or a green Mercedes convertible,
I love my anonymous Buick sedan
which nobody looks at a second time
except when I ferry the women of poetry
down Route Six to the clam shack.

I watch them stroll together
through the old seaside cemetery,
one of them wearing a dead woman's ring,
a cloudy sapphire with a visible flaw,
her ice cream cone leaking
onto the ground where she's paused
to admire a tombstone—
someone's mother has passed away
in the eighty-third year of her age,
someone's beloved husband was lost
to the stormy gray Atlantic—
the same ocean they have floated in,
its bottom matted with grass and hay
whose loose strands clung
to their shoulders and breasts,
the straps of their bathing suits.

They will relax on the veranda
with their black tea
and white cotton robes,
their sailboat hips and unruly hair,
the neighborhood silent

at the edge of the land,
its heirloom tomatoes and horse manure
fragrant under the windows.

They don't need much money
when they go to town,
they like to ride
with the windows down
looking out at the water
and the salt-box houses
and listening to Sarah Vaughn.

For Weldon Kees

Nobody here thinks you really died
having spied you alone on the sidewalk

in New Orleans, full brown moustache
and narrow shoes, the long cuffs
of your linen shirt turned back.

To become as clean as you are—
body of salt, body of glass—
the rest of us would have to sleep
under the desert stars for a year:

Mexico with its funeral horse,
its housefly and cactus, its lottery ticket.

To become as quiet as you are
we would have to originate ourselves
as we do in the fall, watching
more daylight vanish each day,

the crows webbed in shadow
on the garage roof,
the dusky ruinous sunset.

It's the way you lean against
the hotel balcony
sipping a tall grapefruit juice
having grown tired of the sound

of the fountain, dead leaves
blowing past in the street.

You are nobody's father's ghost
spending evenings alone in your room
watching the fan-blades turn overhead
listening to Chopin and Brahms.

Though your absence makes
a dark sea around you
you are not Odysseus,
you are nobody's father.

Night Watchman

He's been waiting a long time to die
the retired security guard
propped in front of the television
crippled, incontinent, gathering his breath
through an oxygen nipple,
his Chevy Caprice with the 350 engine
parked all year by the curb,
and the twelve-gauge he once aimed
at his teenaged grandson
stashed in the bedroom closet.

Though lately he's lived a passive existence
receiving in silence the oatmeal and prunes
from the spoon of his anxious wife,
his big frame collapsed in the armchair
reading Soldier of Fortune,
the lace-up oxfords, cleats on the heels
polished next to the door.
Too sick to work, the Navy checks
spent the first week of the month
on cigarettes and discount Fresca,
powdered eggs and old cowboy movies:

Gene Autry and Randolph Scott
with his long jaw and steely gaze,
his pistols, boots and spurs,
black leather chaps and bandanas,
his gay ass riding tall in the saddle,
or Richard Widmark galloping down Main Street
after robbing the Citizens Bank,

his skin like grained parchment,
his death's-head grin,
his pony kicking up gravel and dust
headed for open range.

Native

Let me say I know nothing
about making lamb stew
watching steam rise from the dark pot
smelling the bayleaf and pepper.
The raven stalks alone through the rain
now that the storm has passed over,
channels of mud slogging the streets,
dahlias bent low and snapped branches
fallen away in the night
which has come again like a lover
to the parking lot next door
of the Narcotics Anonymous meeting,
its car windows and radio antennae.

I've stayed up late listening
to people who no longer speak,
so many gone down
into the black sand of time.
My wife sleeps quietly
in the next room
having told me to let the pot simmer.
And now the night air of autumn
outside the kitchen window.
The hemlock tree and the trumpet vine.
The smoke from the neighbor's chimney.
Even my grandchild's pajamas
drenched on the sagging clothesline:
everything smells like the earth.

Michigan Autumn

This is the glorious wood chalet
where the great Itzhak Perlman stays,
sitting in his wheelchair next to
photos of 17th Century violins
and a poster of Gustav Klimt,
or resting in his deep narrow tub
with its side door through which
he can lower himself to bathe
beneath the shadowy windows
where a funereal wind keeps blowing
banging the shutters closed.

Nobody knows us in these big woods
listening to the creaky
leather-throated wild geese,
the fat year sighing its last overhead,
here where the master cradled the violin,
its ancient varnish, mitres and scrolls.

Soon the winter will step in close
breathing its raw fighter's breath,
thin rain turning to sleet on the railings,
ice in the deepening ruts.
The gold badges of Gustav Klimt
gleam like a pharoah's headdress.
The windows turn dark as this country lake
and the metal canoe upside down on the porch
shines like the lid of a tomb.

The Hustler
for Larry Levis

The bus station's gray light blotching the table
where Paul Newman meets Piper Laurie,
the Ames pool hall window a dusty lens,
the pale talcumed hands of Jackie Gleason, tall cues
poised in their racks, sharp wedge of balls lined up
on its spot, the hunched figures leaning close . . .

most of us are afraid of this shadow
pressing down on the twilit world, the skein
of dingy web over the door, trap
for the housefly and moth. But you watched
these solitary struggles closely, your
gaze undimmed by cruelty or grief.
Marked as you were by the bountiful Sixties
you loved the bright picnic scene too,
where Newman, with casts on both wrists
tells us a man can be an artist at anything,
sunlight redemptive on his T-shirt,
offering the white plaster up to the air.

It's a movie I watched from frayed velour seats
on a Sunday night in Duluth, across the square
from an old casino, mauve fleur-de-lis
on its men's room walls varnished with ancient
cigar smoke and laughter. The croupier's cuff links
shone like blue ice and over the bar in the Gold Room
a young horse painted the colors of daybreak
grazed in a field of dark flowers.

Labor Day

Even the bosses are sleeping late
in the dusty light of September.

The parking lot's empty and no one cares.
No one unloads a ladder, steps on the gas

or starts up the big machines in the shop,
sanding and grinding, cutting and binding.

No one lays a flat bead of flux over a metal seam
or lowers the steel forks from a tailgate.

Shadows gather inside the sleeve
of the empty thermos beside the sink,

the bells go still by the channel buoy,
the wind lies down in the west,

the tuna boats rest on their tie-up lines
turning a little, this way and that.

Day of the Dead

Last night the owl swooped low overhead
and dropped a torn hen carcass
on the neighbor's roof,
red feathers scattered, feet hanging down
which they've left sprawled on the shingles
like some occult sign
hoping to see him return,
and here come the children up the walk
through the pine mulch and drizzle
into my yellow porch light:
Count Dracula with porcelain fangs,
a five-year-old Cleopatra
wearing a vest with gold trim.

All day I've tried to ignore the ice cream truck
jingling its bell past the cemetery
where the tramp in his watch cap sings to himself
like a mad general or movie director:
Jean Cocteau letting the stage dust
filter the twilit underworld
where death looks like a torch singer
who wants to make love to Orpheus,
or Sam Peckinpah with his bullets and dynamite
getting ready to blow up the water tower,
the script in one hand and a gin in the other
keeping an eye out for beauty.

They held my friend's funeral yesterday
out west under the night's long windows,
under its dying stars,

my friend who didn't trust doctors or cops,
who left behind him the green country roads
and the tilted black streets of town,
who left behind the pale flower
whose delicate roots they never could find
blooming inside his brain.

The children paw through the sugar skulls,
their big sister hanging back in the shadows
whispering into her cell phone
like a homicide detective,
the vampire count and Egyptian queen,
history's most famous suicide.
Listen to the night freight coming down,
its engines, its wheels, its sacks of ripe grain,
its gray rats grown fat by the iron tracks,
its love-moan traveling back through the rain.

Notes

On the epigraph page, the Roethke quotation is from his poem "A Walk in Late Summer"; the Neruda quotation is from his poem "Contra-Azul," translated by William O'Daly; and the Neil Young quotation is an album title.

In "Nativity," "So Long It's Been Good to Know You" is a Dust Bowl song by the great Woody Guthrie.

"Ode to the Ear" is for Stephen Kuusisto.

In "Ocean," "Thy sea is so great and my boat is so small" is from the Breton Fisherman's Prayer.

In "Who Do You Love," the quoted lyrics are from the Bo Diddley song of the same name.

"Late December" is for Alan Shapiro.

"Michigan Autumn" is for Jack Driscoll and Michael Delp.

"The Hustler" is Robert Rossen's pool hall film noir circa 1963.

"Day of the Dead" is for David St. John.

Carnegie Mellon Poetry Series
Selected Backlist

2012

Now Make an Altar, Amy Beeder
Still Some Cake, James Cummins
Comet Scar, James Harms
Early Creatures, Native Gods, K.A. Hays
That Was Oasis, Michael McFee
Blue Rust, Joseph Millar
Spitshine, Anne Marie Rooney
Civil Twilight, Margot Schilpp

2011

Having a Little Talk with Capital P Poetry, Jim Daniels
Oz, Nancy Eimers
Working in Flour, Jeff Friedman
Scorpio Rising: Selected Poems, Richard Katrovas
The Politics, Benjamin Paloff
Copperhead, Rachel Richardson

2010

The Diminishing House, Nicky Beer
A World Remembered, T. Alan Broughton
Say Sand, Daniel Coudriet
Knock Knock, Heather Hartley
In the Land We Imagined Ourselves, Jonathan Johnson
Selected Early Poems: 1958-1983, Greg Kuzma
The Other Life: Selected Poems, Herbert Scott
Admission, Jerry Williams

2009

Divine Margins, Peter Cooley
Cultural Studies, Kevin A. González
Dear Apocalypse, K. A. Hays
Warhol-o-rama, Peter Oresick
Group Portrait from Hell, David Schloss
Cave of the Yellow Volkswagen, Maureen Seaton
Birdwatching in Wartime, Jeffrey Thomson

2008

The Grace of Necessity, Samuel Green
After West, James Harms
Anticipate the Coming Reservoir, John Hoppenthaler
Convertible Night, Flurry of Stones, Dzvinia Orlowsky
Parable Hunter, Ricardo Pau-Llosa
The Book of Sleep, Eleanor Stanford

2007

Trick Pear, Suzanne Cleary
So I Will Till the Ground, Gregory Djanikian
Black Threads, Jeff Friedman
Drift and Pulse, Kathleen Halme
The Playhouse Near Dark, Elizabeth Holmes
On the Vanishing of Large Creatures, Susan Hutton
One Season Behind, Sarah Rosenblatt
Indeed I Was Pleased with the World, Mary Ruefle
The Situation, John Skoyles

2006

Burn the Field, Amy Beeder
The Sadness of Others, Hayan Charara

A Grammar to Waking, Nancy Eimers
Dog Star Delicatessen: New and Selected Poems 1979–2006,
　　Mekeel McBride
Shinemaster, Michael McFee
Eastern Mountain Time, Joyce Peseroff
Dragging the Lake, Robert Thomas

2005

Bent to the Earth, Blas Manuel De Luna
Things I Can't Tell You, Michael Dennis Browne
Blindsight, Carol Hamilton
Fallen from a Chariot, Kevin Prufer
Needlegrass, Dennis Sampson
Laws of My Nature, Margot Schilpp
Sleeping Woman, Herbert Scott
Renovation, Jeffrey Thomson

2004

The Women Who Loved Elvis All Their Lives, Fleda Brown
The Chronic Liar Buys a Canary, Elizabeth Edwards
Freeways and Aqueducts, James Harms
Prague Winter, Richard Katrovas
Trains in Winter, Jay Meek
Tristimania, Mary Ruefle
Venus Examines Her Breast, Maureen Seaton
Various Orbits, Thom Ward

2003

Trouble, Mary Baine Campbell
A Place Made of Starlight, Peter Cooley
Taking Down the Angel, Jeff Friedman

Lives of Water, John Hoppenthaler
Imitation of Life, Allison Joseph
Except for One Obscene Brushstroke, Dzvinia Orlowsky
The Mastery Impulse, Ricardo Pau-Llosa
Casino of the Sun, Jerry Williams

2002

Keeping Time, Suzanne Cleary
Astronaut, Brian Henry
What it Wasn't, Laura Kasischke
Slow Risen Among the Smoke Trees, Elizabeth Kirschner
The Finger Bone, Kevin Prufer
Among the Musk Ox People, Mary Ruefle
The Late World, Arthur Smith

2001

Day Moon, Jon Anderson
The Origin of Green, T. Alan Broughton
Lovers in the Used World, Gillian Conoley
Quarters, James Harms
Mastodon, 80% Complete, Jonathan Johnson
The Deepest Part of the River, Mekeel McBride
Earthly, Michael McFee
Ten Thousand Good Mornings, James Reiss
The World's Last Night, Margot Schilpp
Sex Lives of the Poor and Obscure, David Schloss
Glacier Wine, Maura Stanton
Voyages in English, Dara Wier

2000

Blue Jesus, Jim Daniels

Years Later, Gregory Djanikian

Mortal Education, Joyce Peseroff

How Things Are, James Richardson

On the Waterbed They Sank to Their Own Levels, Sarah Rosenblatt

Post Meridian, Mary Ruefle

Constant Longing, Dennis Sampson

Hierarchies of Rue, Roger Sauls

Small Boat with Oars of Different Size, Thom Ward

Winter Morning Walks: 100 Postcards to Jim Harrison, Ted Kooser